XTREME SPORTS

Summer

by Joe Layden

XTREME SPORTS

Summer

by Joe Layden

SCHOLASTIC INC.

New York   Toronto   London   Auckland   Sydney
Mexico City   New Delhi   Hong Kong   Buenos Aires

ISBN 0-439-52217-X

12 11 10   9/0
                                                                                                   40

Printed in the U.S.A.
First printing, March 2003
Book Design: Michael Malone

TABLE of CONTENTS

INTRODUCTION

What makes an athlete great?

Is it courage? Talent? Ambition? Maybe it's some combination of the three. This much is for sure: all of the men and women you'll find on the pages of this book are extraordinary individuals who have devoted their lives to their sports. It doesn't matter that the games they play aren't necessarily the kind your parents played. The world has changed, and so has the definition of the word "sport." Just because someone chooses skateboarding over soccer, or BMX over baseball, doesn't mean he's not serious about his athletic career. Just ask anyone who has ever won a gold medal at the X Games. Success does not come without a price. As in any sport, you reach the

Eito Yasutoko

peak only through endless hours of training. Sure, they make it look like fun, and it is! But it's also hard work. If you want to be the best, there are no shortcuts.

Take the Yasutoko brothers, for example. They are masters of the vert ramp in aggressive in-line skating. Younger brother

Takeshi skates with the fluidity and grace of a dancer. Older brother Eito is less subtle. He attacks the ramp, wringing every ounce of energy from his body. Each has a unique style of performing and competing. But in the quiet times, when no one is watching, they work as hard as any professional athlete. They train for hours on end, without a break. They endure aching muscles and an occasional cracked bone. Because there is no alternative...not even in the world of alternative sports.

As Ken Bradshaw says, "It all comes down to desire."

Who is Ken Bradshaw? He's a legend in surfing, perhaps the original extreme sport. He's also a role model for anyone who hopes to have a long career doing something he truly loves. You see, at 50 years of age, Ken is older than most of your parents.

**As Ken Bradshaw says,
"It all comes down to desire."**

But he's still capable of riding the biggest waves on the planet. Check out his story and you'll be amazed.

But then, that's true of everyone in this book: surfers Lisa Anderson and Ken Bradshaw, the Yasutoko brothers, skateboarders Bob Burnquist and Andy Macdonald, freestyle motocross daredevil Carey Hart, BMX champ Ryan Nyquist, wakeboarder Emily Copeland. They are all remarkable athletes who have made sacrifices to achieve greatness. But they don't mind, because they love what they're doing.

Lisa ANDERSON

DATE OF BIRTH: MARCH 8, 1969

Lisa Anderson may have the good looks of a model, but in her heart she's still a tomboy. The first lady of surfing was the only girl on her Little League baseball team, and when she traded in her bat for a board, she quickly discovered that the secret to success was competing against the best athletes she could find. More often than not, she was the only girl in the water. And she didn't mind in the least.

"I've never been very impressed with the way most women surf," Lisa told *Surf Life for Women* magazine. "When you compare them with men, it's like night and day. I'd only been surfing a very short time when I began to believe I had the potential to be as good or better than any other woman surfer. I knew I'd limit myself if I surfed with other girls, so I surfed with the guys."

That strategy paid off, for Lisa became surfing's first female superstar. She's won four world championships (only Australian Layne Beachley has matched that accomplishment) and opened countless doors for other women. Today, some of the most popular and successful athletes in surfing are female, and they all have Lisa Anderson to thank.

● ●

"When I was a kid, all I wanted to do was surf. I just wanted to go to the water and jump in."

● ●

As *Wahine* magazine noted, "Lisa not only raised the technical ability of women in surfing, she raised the sponsorship money."

If not for the fact that her family moved from Virginia to Florida when she was in junior high school, Lisa might never have discovered surfing. Her introduction to the sport came at the age of 14, on a summer morning in Ormond Beach. Lisa paddled a friend's surfboard out into

A CHANGE OF HEART

Surfing once drove a wedge between Lisa and her parents. But now Lisa's mother loves the sport. "I was all wrong about surfing," she says. "I don't know where Lisa would be without it."

some small waves and waited for an opportunity to ride. To the surprise of her friend, and everyone else on the beach, Lisa caught the first wave perfectly, stood up on her board, and rode it all the way into shore. She was a natural!

Lisa soon became the only girl on the Seabreeze High School surfing team. Her neon-pink surfboard was the target of many jokes among her teammates, but Lisa's talent was no laughing matter. She was the star of the team. To fit in with the guys, she adopted a tough attitude, which sometimes got her in trouble. In fact, "Trouble" became Lisa's nickname.

Despite her success in surfing, Lisa's teenage years weren't easy. Her parents were going through a messy divorce, and Lisa used surfing as a way to escape the harshness of her home

It's a Man's World

In 1997 Lisa competed in surfing's U.S. Open. She was the only woman in a field of 360 competitors.

life. Sometimes she would stay out late at night. She'd skip school and spend the whole day hanging out at the beach, searching for the perfect wave. Lisa's parents became angry with her. They became convinced that surfing was the root of her problems. One day, in fact, Lisa's father became so angry that he took her surfboard and stomped on it, smashing the fin.

"We associated surfing with drugs and beach bums," Lisa's mother, Lorraine Lemelin, later explained in an interview with *Outside* magazine. "It didn't seem like a good lifestyle for a young woman. Lisa was headstrong, always hanging out with older kids. She gave me more trouble than any of her three brothers."

Things got so bad that Lisa eventually ran away from home. She was only 16 years old at the time. Before leaving, she wrote a note to her mother. Lisa assured her mother that she had a plan. She was going to California to train. Someday, she promised, she would be the world champion of women's surfing.

"That was really just a line I fed my mom," Lisa admits. "I didn't even know if there was a world championship in women's surfing. But I wanted to make leaving home sound good. I wanted her to think I was doing it for a good reason. And, I guess, there was a part of me that wanted to be the best."

A big part, as it turned out. Lisa landed in Huntington Beach, California. She supported herself by working as a waitress. All of her spare time was spent at the beach. Lisa quickly became one of the top amateur surfers in the United States. She won more than thirty tournaments in less than a year. After winning the 1987 U.S. Amateur Championships, she decided to turn professional. Lisa made just as big a splash in the pro ranks, winning Rookie of the Year honors. She was only nineteen years old, and already she was one of the top female surfers in the world.

But then Lisa's career stalled. Sometimes she

surfed with confidence. Other times she was unsure of herself. Although she was considered one of the most talented surfers on the pro tour, Lisa surfed for five years before finally winning an event.

"I still have a hard time understanding everything I did wrong and what took me so long to pull it all together," Lisa says. "I blame a lot of my early problems on a lack of focus. I'd be surfing really well in practice, and then I'd turn into a kook right before competitions. It was an incredibly frustrating experience."

Everything changed for Lisa in 1992, when she began training with a man named Tom Carroll, himself a two-time world champion. He helped Lisa improve her technique. She also worked hard to improve her conditioning. Lisa had always gotten by on natural ability and talent. Now she was working as hard as anyone on the pro tour, and the results were impressive. Lisa won three events in 1992 and finished fourth in the overall standings. She was an overwhelming favorite to win the title in 1993, but the birth of her first daughter, Erica, forced Lisa to alter her plans.

"I was all set to go for the title," Lisa recalls. "And then Erica came along. But she made me a better and more complete person."

Being a single mom on the pro surfing tour wasn't easy. Erica traveled everywhere with Lisa. Mom would play with her daughter on the beach, interrupting their time together just long

• •

"I blame a lot of my early problems on a lack of focus. I'd be surfing really well in practice, and then I'd turn into a kook right before competitions. It was an incredibly frustrating experience."

• •

enough to compete in a heat. Amazingly enough, Lisa soon regained her form. She won her first overall tour title in 1994, despite suffering from severe back spasms that forced her to miss a pair of events late in the year. In 1995 she repeated as champion. That accomplishment prompted *Surfer* magazine to put Lisa on the cover of its April 1996 issue. She was only the second woman so honored in the magazine's 40-year history. Of course, Lisa deserved it. She won a third straight championship in 1996 and a fourth in 1997. By that time Lisa was no longer just the best female surfer in the world. She was one of the best surfers in history—period!

"Having children, and being responsible for them, motivates me to be my best and to do my best. My daughter drove me to win the title in 1994."

Injuries and family commitments prevented Lisa from winning a fifth straight title, but she remained one of the tour's best surfers—and one of the sport's most popular athletes—into the twenty-first century. She's also made peace with her past. Lisa and her mother have made up. In fact, the two even live together in Florida! Lisa's second child, Mason, was born in 2001, so she's busier than ever. But at 33 years of age, Lisa isn't ready to hang up her surfboard. She's train-

ing hard and plans to return to the pro tour as soon as possible.

"I'm not ready to retire," Lisa says. "Not yet."

Ken BRADSHAW

DATE OF BIRTH: OCTOBER 4, 1952

You think extreme sports are only for the young? If so, then you've obviously never met Ken Bradshaw. Here's a man who recently turned 50 years old and yet remains one of the most accomplished athletes in the world. Ken celebrated his birthday not with a big wedge of cake or a leisurely round of golf. He's far too much of a fitness nut for anything like that. Instead, he spent the day doing what he loves best: paddling into rugged water on his surfboard and racing toward the beach like a bullet.

You see, no one tracks big waves quite like Ken Bradshaw. He's traveled all over the world in search of wild and dangerous surf, and more often than not he's found it. In 1998, for example, Ken set a world record by riding a wave that measured more than 80 feet across its face! Imagine surfing along the top of an eight-story building and you get the picture. It's practically impossible, and yet Ken did it. Even more amazing is the fact that he was 45 years old when he accomplished this feat. The best surfers in the world are half Ken's age, and most of them would not even attempt such a ride. He's the grandfather of extreme surfing, and he can still teach the kids a lesson or two.

• •

"I'm totally into procedures and rules. We run a tight ship in my group."

• •

"Ken has the passion, the desire, and the incredible fearless attitude it takes to live his dreams," says his close friend, world champion surfer Layne Beachley. "Some people think he's a little crazy, but I think he's a true inspiration."

Maybe he's both. A lot of people thought NBA superstar Michael Jordan was crazy for attempting a comeback. And Michael wasn't

even 40 years old. Ken Bradshaw, at 50, is still the best at what he does. And make no mistake, what he does is both dangerous and demanding. Most people would also consider it terrifying. But not Ken.

"I don't measure my experiences in big waves as scary," he told **EXPN.com**. "As long as you're mentally and physically prepared for the inevitable outcome of wiping out or having to swim to shore, you feel much more secure. It's funny. I've been beat up so badly that it becomes like normal behavior. If you're afraid to get pounded, you shouldn't be out there."

If anyone is suited to big-wave surfing, it's Ken. He's devoted his entire life to the sport, and thanks to a rigorous training routine, combined

• •

"People who surf big waves on a regular basis don't consider it a death-defying act. We don't keep the danger in our minds at all. I've had 30 years of experience to achieve at this level, so to me, it's fun."

• •

with a healthy diet, he remains as fit as any world-class athlete. He runs a very successful company that designs and markets surfboards, and younger surfers often ask him for coaching advice. In other words, no one knows more about surfing than Ken.

Of course, that wasn't the case back in the

late 1960s, when Ken first felt the bite of the surfing bug, which didn't exactly sit well with his family. Ken's father was a military veteran who had built a company that produced tools for the oil business. He was a tough and busy man who worked hard to make a good living.

The Bradshaw family moved around a lot and eventually settled in Houston, Texas. Like most athletic kids from the Lone Star State, Ken played football. He was good at it, too. The intensity and athleticism that would eventually make him a great surfer were evident on the football field. By the time he was in tenth grade, Ken was nearly six feet tall and weighed 170 pounds. He was one of the best linebackers in the city. College scouts were drooling over him. It was apparent that Ken could play big-time football, and a college scholarship seemed to be his for the taking.

There was just one problem. Ken didn't want to play football. And he didn't want to go to college. In fact, once Ken got a taste of surfing during a weekend trip to Surfside, Texas, on the Gulf Coast, he lost interest in just about every-

MEDIA MAGNET

Few surfers have enjoyed as much publicity as Ken. He has been featured on dozens of national televison shows, including *20/20*, *ABC's Wide World of Sports*, and special segments on National Geographic, Fox and NBC. He's also been profiled in such national publications as *Vanity Fair*, *Rolling Stone* and *Outside*, in addition to all of the major surfing magazines.

thing except surfing. That didn't exactly make his family happy.

"Football was fun, no doubt about it," Ken says. "But I loved surfing. I'd stay out there in the water for ten hours straight. I got so into surfing a couple of summers that my parents just couldn't handle it. I didn't want to play football anymore, and for them, that was it. We started fighting. I actually ran away from home twice."

The first time he returned. The second time, when he was 17, Ken ran away for good. He wound up in California, which was the surfing capital of the continental United States. Ken loved California. The waves were bigger and more consistent, and it seemed like everyone owned a surfboard. He surfed every day and learned a lot about the sport. After a couple years he decided he was ready to make another move, this time to Hawaii.

Hawaii, located far out in the Pacific Ocean, is a surfer's paradise. Many of the best athletes in the sport grew up there, and many others have moved there to train. The water is warm, the weather beautiful, and the waves are some of the biggest on the planet. If you're serious about surfing, then Hawaii is the place to be. And Ken was a very serious young man.

In 1972 he moved to Hawaii. He worked at a variety of jobs, usually in the tourism industry. Determined not to be recognized as a dropout, Ken earned a high school equivalency diploma. And, of course, he surfed. Hour after hour, day after day, until his body ached and his skin was as withered as a prune's.

"It took two full years in Hawaii for me to get

used to the surf," Ken recalls. "You can't go over there expecting to just tear it down right away. It takes time."

Ken had the patience and ambition to become a great surfer. Not long after arriving in Hawaii he realized that his natural toughness would take him only so far. So he became a true student of the sport. Ken wanted to learn everything about surfing, so he watched tapes of the great champions. He devoured their autobiographies. And he learned how to read the ocean.

Eventually Ken began competing in major surfing contests, including the world championships. He won the legendary Duke Kahanamoku Classic in 1982, which boosted his reputation and led to sponsorship deals with some of the biggest companies in the surfing industry. For most men, this would have been enough. But Ken is not an ordinary guy. He has boundless energy. So he started making and selling his own surfboards. And he worked as a stuntman in the movie industry.

By the mid-1980s Ken had become less interested in traditional surfing contests. His focus was big-wave surfing. In 1986 he tried to paddle into a giant wave at a place called Outside Log Cabins, on the notoriously rough North Shore of Hawaii. But the waves were too big and too fast. They kept washing over Ken

Physically Fit

Ken knows that in order to withstand the rigors of big-wave surfing, he has to be in great shape. That's why he takes care of his body. Ken is a strict vegetarian and does not drink alcohol or take any drugs.

and his board. Still, Ken was determined to ride one of these giants. He just wasn't sure how to do it without getting killed.

The answer came a few years later, when surfers began using personal watercraft, such as Jet Skis, to ride bigger waves. Ken was at the forefront of this movement. He became one of the first surfers to master the art of what is commonly known as "tow-in" surfing, in which the surfer is pulled into the wave at a high rate of speed. It is, according to Ken, the only way to ride the tallest waves.

"There is no way you can successfully paddle

into a 40-foot wave," Ken says. "It's too thick, too fast, and there's too much water. You'll get swallowed."

Tow-in surfing is still very risky, especially since it encourages athletes to tackle bigger challenges. Like the one Ken accepted on January 28, 1998. It was on that day that he returned to Outside Log Cabins. Accompanied by a documentary film crew working on an IMAX project called Extreme, Ken did what no one had ever done. He surfed an 80-foot wave. And he didn't even wipe out!

"I knew it was huge," Ken later explained. "But I didn't realize how big until I saw some video that night. It was ten times overhead and there was still plenty of water under my board. Looking up, it was the most phenomenal thing I have ever seen."

Ken hasn't ridden another wave that large. But then, neither has anyone else. And maybe they never will. Because there is only one Ken Bradshaw.

Bob BURNQUIST

He may not get quite as much publicity as some skateboarders, but if you ask any of his fellow competitors, they'll tell you that Bob Burnquist is the best in the business. Not only is he one the few athletes who can perform almost any trick using either a regular or switch stance, but he's also one of the most creative skaters around. You see, Bob has the soul of an artist and the heart of a competitor. That's why he's respected by his peers and admired by skateboarding fans all over the world.

Listen to what Tony Hawk, the most famous and popular of all extreme sports athletes, has to say about Bob: "In vert skating, Bob is pushing the envelope. He's changing what we consider to be possible."

That's high praise, and it's why skateboard publications routinely place Bob at the top of their rankings. "He's hands-down the most innovative skater in the world," wrote *Thrasher* magazine in the spring of 2002. "Bob is ten years

• •

"I didn't have many insecurities in high school because I was so different anyway. I had blue hair and I was a skateboarder. Nobody really liked me, so I was like, 'I don't care.'"

• •

ahead of everyone else. Inventing tricks is a rarity these days in skateboarding, but Bob seems to have a new one at every contest."

Born in Rio de Janeiro, Brazil, Bob grew up in a multicultural family. His father is American. His mother is Brazilian. Bob, naturally, learned to speak two languages as a boy: English and Portuguese (the language commonly spoken in Brazil). He started skating when he was ten years old on the streets of Sao Paulo (the capital of

Brazil). Back then, skateboarding didn't have much of a following in Brazil, and there were very few vert ramps or skate parks. But that didn't matter to Bob.

"Skating was all I did," he recalls. "I rode twenty-four/seven. Once I got on that skateboard, I never wanted to leave it again."

A Man of Many Talents

Bob doesn't like to sit still for long. When he gets tired of skating, he just turns to one of his many hobbies, including surfing, snowboarding and BMX.

In some ways, Bob has said, that was a big advantage for him. He didn't follow skateboarding trends the way some young athletes did. Although he studied videotapes of some of the world's top skaters, such as Hawk and Colin McKay, he didn't try to copy what he saw. Instead, he took pieces of their best moves and blended them with his own to create a unique style that often included skating switch stance (backward). And once he'd learned how to skate on handrails and in empty swimming pools, as well as on city streets dotted with potholes, he knew he could handle almost anything. To Bob, the best part of skating was meeting new challenges and inventing new tricks. It became an outlet for his creative energy.

"Skateboarding gives me direction," Bob told *Transworld Skateboarding* magazine. "It gives me motivation to live. I just know that with skateboarding I can accomplish anything I set my mind to. It's a way to express myself, a way to release what I feel."

As an athlete, Bob developed largely in private. Although he got his first sponsor (a Brazilian clothing company) when he was 14, it wasn't until May of 1995 that the rest of the world got a glimpse of his awesome talent. Bob's debut came at the Slam City Jam skateboarding contest in Vancouver, Canada. He showed up wearing knee-high white tube socks and a goofy grin. It wasn't a look that sent fear into the hearts of his opponents. But the minute Bob stepped onto his board, everything changed. He was just 17 years old at the time, but he skated like a veteran. Actually, that isn't quite true, because no one had ever performed the way Bob did that day. Using the switch stance more commonly seen in park and street skating, Bob glided up and down the vert ramp. He soared high into the air and turned his body into something resembling a corkscrew. His moves and tricks seemed

•••••••••••••••••••••••••••••••

"Moving to the United States helped me a lot. Skating with all the great skaters here just really got me progressing. It makes a big difference when you have other skaters pushing you to go further."

•••••••••••••••••••••••••••••••

similar to those performed by Hawk and others, but they looked completely different.

The crowd in Vancouver was overwhelmed—and a bit confused. They'd never seen anyone skate the way Bob skated. By the time he was finished, Bob had a gold medal. He was the new star of professional skateboarding!

"I wasn't expecting to win anything," Bob said afterward. "Maybe that's why I did so well."

Or perhaps it was because Bob's radical approach to skating stunned the judges as much

as it stunned the fans. Skateboarding had fallen into a bit of a rut in the early 1990s, and Bob's innovative, emotional approach helped give the sport new life. He wasn't content to simply mimic other skaters. And he still isn't.

"Having a good time and learning new tricks is what keeps me skating," Bob told **EXPN.com**.

MONKEY BUSINESS

In 2002 Bob worked on a movie called *MVP2: Most Vertical Primate*. His job was to give skateboarding lessons to the movie's star: a chimpanzee!

"It gets harder and harder to get that certain feeling you get after doing something for the first time. But that's what I like about skating."

Bob is best known for being one of the most creative and unique skaters in the world. He spends a lot of his time dreaming up moves that seem almost impossible, just because he enjoys it so much. Bob is a competitor, too. He's won seven medals in vert at the Summer X Games, including two gold. And he's a two-time world champion. But he's also a fan. If you go to a big-time skateboarding competition it won't be hard to pick him out of the crowd. He'll be the one running all over the place, shouting encouragement to his fellow skaters and applauding for them when they execute difficult tricks. Bob is a genuinely nice guy who appreciates a good performance, even if it costs him a victory.

That attitude, combined with his extraordinary talent, has made Bob one of the most popular extreme sports athletes in the world today. *Thrasher* named him skater of the year in 1997. The following year, in a riders' poll conducted by *Transworld*, he was voted best vert skater and best overall skater. Those awards were special, because they were determined by a vote of Bob's peers. In 1999 he crossed over into the mainstream, earning a spot on *Rolling Stone* magazine's list of the top athletes of the year.

Although he's lived in the United States since he was 17, Bob still feels a tremendous connection to his homeland, which he visits at least five or six times a year. His success is widely considered to be one of the main reasons that some of the top skaters in the world now come from Brazil. When kids like 2002 X Games champ Rodil de Araujo, Jr. were growing up, they dreamed of following in Bob's footsteps. That he has served as an inspiration pleases Bob almost as much as nailing a new trick.

"There's a whole Brazilian army of skateboarders, and now we have a lot of respect," Bob told *Sports Illustrated for Kids.* "When people talk about Brazilians, they go, 'Oh, wow, yeah.' When before it was, 'Acckkk!' It's quite different than it was ten years ago. There used to be a really harsh environment for Brazilian skaters, but we started breaking barriers and opening doors. It feels really good to have helped, but in no way am I the sole person responsible."

In addition to being a great skater, Bob is a smart and successful businessman who owns an organic food company and a popular restaurant in California. He also has a young daughter named Lotus. So there isn't a lot of free time in Bob's life. Somehow, though, he always makes room for skateboarding. In fact, Bob even has a 123-foot-long halfpipe, along with a loop, in his own backyard! He skates there whenever he's home. And if anyone stops by with a board tucked under their arm, they're welcome to join him.

"It's a dream come true," Bob says of his private skate park. "It's heaven on earth for a skate-

boarder. And since it is heaven on earth, I don't charge anyone to skate. If I'm around and there are people around to skate in the neighborhood, they come by and we all skate together."

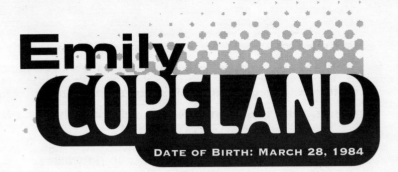

Emily COPELAND

DATE OF BIRTH: MARCH 28, 1984

For someone about to compete in the most important event of her life, Emily Copeland sure didn't look too concerned. This was just a few minutes before the start of the women's wakeboarding final at the 2002 Summer X Games, and Emily was laughing and doing handstands along the banks of the Schuylkill River in Philadelphia. Not only that, but so was her chief rival and training partner, Dallas Friday, the defending X Games champion.

Did someone forget to tell these young women exactly what was at stake?

"Nah, that's just something we like to do," Emily later explained. "We always have those handstand competitions. To be honest, I was pretty nervous."

That's one of the interesting things about Emily. The two-time world wakeboarding champion is a talented and driven athlete, but she always manages to keep things in perspective.

"Not many people get the chance to do what I'm doing," Emily told **Crosswalk.com**. "I'm trav-

• •

"As long as I'm wakeboarding, my goal will be to be the best. I look at this as my job, and I take it very seriously."

• •

eling all over the world and I'm making a living off something that I love, so it's really a cool thing. I never thought I would have this opportunity. I'm lucky."

Emily didn't set out to be one of the biggest stars in wakeboarding. It just sort of happened. She grew up in Denver, Colorado, the youngest of three children in a close-knit and highly active family. Colorado, of course, is snow country, so all the Copeland children enjoyed skiing and snowboarding. But Emily's favorite sport

was gymnastics. Like many girls, she began tumbling and leaping when she was barely old enough to walk. She dreamed of being an Olympic champion, the next Mary Lou Retton or Keri Strug.

Though Emily had talent, she wasn't really ideally suited for gymnastics. Gymnasts are typically short and muscular. Emily was long and lean (she's now 5-foot-9). Still, she wasn't easily discouraged. She continued to practice and improve. It wasn't until she was 13 years old that Emily decided to make a change to wakeboarding. All because of a brother who wouldn't take no for an answer.

Bart Copeland was by that time already one of the top wakeboarders in the world. He had seen Emily working out in the gym, and he had watched her gliding smoothly down the side of a mountain on a snowboard. It occurred to Bart that his little sister had exactly the right combination of skills to excel at the sport he loved. Wakeboarding, after all, is like a combination of snowboarding and waterskiing. Participants are towed behind a boat while strapped onto a board with fins. They perform spins and jumps and flips at speeds approaching 30 miles per hour. Sometimes they even use ramps (known as sliders) to catch big air over the water, which really makes the sport exciting. And a little bit dangerous. The way Bart saw it, there was no better preparation for an aspiring wakeboarder

NOW THAT'S GROSS!

If you saw any of the wakeboarding competitors making strange faces during their runs at the 2002 X Games, it may not have been because they were tired or sore. It may have been the water in the Schuylkill River, which wasn't exactly crystal clear. "It's really nasty, actually," Emily said. "Afterward they tell us to wash our ears out with alcohol."

than gymnastics and snowboarding.

And anyway, he figured it had to be more fun than being cooped up in a gym all day.

"Bart really wanted me to get into it," Emily recalls. "So he talked me into trying it one day. I think within my first week I was landing flips, and it just kind of took off from there."

There were, of course, more than a few painful slips and falls, too. In fact, even though she really enjoyed the new sport, Emily did a lot of complaining those first few weeks. She even threatened to quit. But Bart wouldn't let her. He

ROLE MODEL

Emily is well aware of the growing popularity of extreme sports, and the impact she can have on the young members of her audience. Especially girls. "It's a huge thing to have this opportunity," she says. "And when you have young girls looking up to you, you feel like you have to make sure you're being good and setting a good example."

could tell right away that his little sister had big-time potential as a wakeboarder.

"I was never a natural like her," Bart told the *Denver Post*. "I had all the tricks, but I could never make it stand up in competition and be consistent. That's one thing about Emily: she's so consistent and calm under pressure. She's pushing women's wakeboarding to a whole different level."

Bart would know. A year after being introduced to the sport, Emily left Colorado and moved to Florida to live and train with her brother. Her devotion to the sport was apparent from the start. As was her talent. In 1999 Emily became only the second woman to win the Pro Wakeboard Tour championship in her rookie season. The first was Tara Hamilton, who was among the veterans chasing Emily that season. But none could catch her. At just 15 years of age Emily was already one of the most accomplished wakeboarders in the world!

"It all happened pretty quickly for me," Emily says. "I really wasn't going many places with gymnastics. Then wakeboarding came along and the timing was perfect."

With such rapid improvement came notoriety and confidence. Thanks to her Pro Wakeboard Tour title, Emily escaped the long shadow cast by her brother. In fact, Bart retired from competitive wakeboarding last year, at the age of 23. But he remains Emily's biggest fan.

"It's just cool to watch her out there," Bart says proudly. "She is so skilled."

Despite her youth and relative lack of experience, Emily has been the most dominant rider in the sport over the past three years. She captured the Pro Wakeboard Tour title again in 2001, as well as the U.S. Open, U.S. Masters and Wakeboard World Championship titles. In July of 2002 she finished first at the Gravity Games. About the only honor that had eluded Emily in her first three years of pro competition was a gold medal at the X Games, widely considered to

"Losing is not easy, but it's definitely something that comes with competing. I mean, you're not going to have your best day every day. So you just have to learn to handle it and realize that there's always going to be a next time."

be the most prestigious of alternative sports festivals. She had taken silver twice, in 1999 and 2001, but never gold. Although she didn't say much about it, Emily was determined to fill that hole on her resume in 2002.

So, after she had finished warming up with a few handstands, Emily got down to business. She rode flawlessly, completing a series of dazzling tricks, including a 540-degree roll while nearly parallel to the water. Dallas rode well, too, but when the scores were announced, Emily was the winner. Finally she was an X Games champion!

"Everybody around the world knows what the X Games is," Emily said afterward. "To take home the gold has been a huge goal of mine. When I heard that I won, I couldn't believe it. I still can't believe it. I'm speechless."

But not for long. As the brightest young star in professional wakeboarding, Emily has become a very busy young woman. She has numerous sponsorship deals, including one with Nike, and has been featured in such national magazines as *Sports Illustrated*. With her ever-present smile and outgoing personality, Emily is sure to become one of the most popular athletes in extreme sports. And the really scary part is, she's only going to get better. You see, at 18 years of age, Emily is just getting warmed up.

"I plan to be around for at least another five years," she says. "I've been able to watch the sport evolve and grow, and I think it's all become

● ●

**"Everybody around the world
knows what the X Games is.
To take home the gold has been
a huge goal of mine. When I
heard that I won, I couldn't
believe it."**

● ●

pretty cool. It's been an awesome experience to see how far the women have come and how far the sport has come. Hopefully I'll be looked back on as one of the innovators of the sport. That would be nice."

Carey HART

DATE OF BIRTH: JULY 17, 1975

Things are not always what they appear to be.

Take freestyle motocross superstar Carey Hart, for example. Here's a guy with a Mohawk hairdo, an ever-present scowl, a rock star girlfriend, and more tattoos than Allen Iverson. He seems to be trying awfully hard to play the role of the extreme sports tough guy.

But nothing could be further from the truth. Take a closer look and you'll see a guy utterly devoted to his friends, his family and his sport. You'll also find a guy who has the ability to laugh at himself, even when he's in a lot of pain. Carey was once asked what went through his mind as he attempted a failed backflip on his motorcycle at the 2001 X Games. He smiled, laughed, and said, "Uh, I was thinking about whether I was going to splat like a pancake. I was falling from pretty high, so I just wanted to do as little damage as possible."

Carey actually did quite a lot of damage that day. But then, injuries are commonplace in the dangerous world of freestyle motocross, so there's nothing unique about the assortment of broken bones and torn ligaments Carey has amassed over the years. What is unusual is the life he has led, and the relationships he has maintained.

● ●

"I learned how to ride a motorcycle before I learned how to ride a regular bike. I was just having fun."

● ●

Carey grew up in Las Vegas, Nevada. He started riding dirt bikes when he was just four years old. His father taught him how to ride. Tom Hart was a single parent who did his best to give Carey a happy and stable home. In the case of the Hart family, one of the secrets to happi-

ness was spending as much time as possible outdoors in the fresh air, on the back of a motorcycle or minibike.

"I learned how to ride a motorcycle before I learned how to ride a regular bike," Carey told **EXPN.com**. "I was just having fun."

Carey had a lot of talent, as well as a desire

to compete, so he naturally gravitated toward racing. He was pretty good at it, too. He turned professional at the age of 17 and made his living as a racer for the next six years. But eventually Carey became more interested in freestyle motocross, with its emphasis on creativity and

● ●

"I've never been too big into freestyle contest results and all that. I just want to push things and keep making progress."

● ●

style. He soon became one of the most popular and successful performers on the freestyle circuit. Carey was great at inventing new tricks. And in a sport that prized courage, he seemed almost fearless.

Of course, in freestyle motocross, there is a fine line between bravery and foolishness. When you're flying 50 feet in the air on a 220-pound motorcycle, at speeds approaching 70 miles per hour, there is almost no room for error. Freestyle is still a relatively new sport, and each year the athletes have gotten a little better, the tricks a little wilder, the stakes a little higher. No one knows that better than Carey.

At the 2000 Gravity Games, Carey became the first person to land a backflip in competition. Well, almost. The truth is, Carey landed hard and fell off his bike after attempting the move. In the process, he suffered a compressed

• •

"I think it's great that everybody is trying the backflip now. It's constant progression and that's what the sport needs. I'm not the kind of person who would be bummed with other people doing it. That's just not my nature."

• •

vertebra and torn ligaments in his lower back. Some people never gave Carey credit for making history on that day. They claimed that since he failed to stay on his bike, he didn't really complete a backflip, which was considered to be the most difficult and dangerous trick in freestyle motocross.

But Carey wasn't discouraged or disappointed. Instead he became more determined than ever

to execute a backflip—a trick he called the "Hart Breaker." A full year passed before Carey tried again. A full year during which no one else had the guts to attempt a backflip. But Carey did. At the 2001 X Games in Philadelphia, Carey stunned a packed house at the First Union Center with another full, floating backflip in the freestyle motocross competition. Unfortunately, this time Carey didn't come close. He lost control of his bike and had to bail out. Carey fell 40 feet to the ground, and lay motionless for several minutes before being helped off the course and taken to a hospital. His injuries were severe but not life-threatening: a broken foot, a few cracked ribs, and a bruised tailbone.

During his first few months of rehabilitation, Carey said he would never attempt another backflip. But as his body healed, he began to change his mind. Before long Carey was practicing the trick again, using mountains of foam and padding to soften his fall whenever he failed, which, of course, was most of the time. Carey still wanted to land a backflip, but he knew other riders were practicing just as hard.

IN THE SHADOWS

Carey is pretty well known in the world of extreme sports, but when he hangs out with his girlfriend, Pink, it's clear which one is the bigger celebrity. But that's okay with Carey. He doesn't mind giving up the spotlight. "She's so level-headed, and I'm not like a rock star or anything," Carey says. "Everywhere we go, she is recognized, but I like being a bit in the background."

The backflip had become the most prized trick in all of freestyle motocross. Everyone wanted a piece of it.

Unfortunately, Carey couldn't concentrate entirely on his riding. He had other things on his mind, like the health of his father. Tom Hart was battling cancer for most of 2001 and 2002. Carey, who considers his father to be his best friend, was right by Tom's side all the way. He even shaved his hair into a Mohawk as a tribute to his father.

"My dad has always been there for me," Carey

says. "He's done so much. When he came down with cancer and had to go through chemotherapy, I tried to lighten the blow a bit. I said I'd grow the Mohawk until he kicked cancer."

"My dad has always been there for me. He's done so much. When he came down with cancer and had to go through chemotherapy, I tried to lighten the blow a bit. I said I'd grow the Mohawk until he kicked cancer."

Tom's cancer went into remission in July of 2002. One month later father and son were back in Philadelphia for the Summer X Games. Carey competed only in the big air competition, on the final night of the Games. By that time Mike Metzger had already broken new ground by landing consecutive backflips in the freestyle competition. But Carey still had a goal. He wanted to prove to himself and to everyone else in the motocross world that he could stick the backflip, too. And that's precisely what he did.

To heighten the tension, Carey skipped the

first two rounds of the big air competition. That meant his final score would be based on a single jump. Carey hadn't told the media whether he would try another backflip, but most people assumed that he would. As Carey straddled his bike at the top of the ramp, concentrating on the most important jump of his life, the crowd held its breath. Everyone in Carey's support crew was nervous, including his famous girlfriend, pop singer Pink, who had interrupted a tour and chartered a jet to Philadelphia so that she could be with Carey on one of the biggest nights of his life.

Carey hit the throttle and roared down the ramp. He soared into the air, pulled lightly on the handlebars, tilted his head back, and rotated through a perfect backflip. The landing was a bit rough, but this time he stayed on his bike. In fact, Carey leaned into the throttle again and drove away, pumping his fists with delight. A few moments later the First Union Center went wild as Carey's score flashed on the screen overhead: 94.67 out of 100. Only Mike Metzger, the godfather of freestyle motocross and a good friend of Carey's, had done better. Carey was now an X Games silver medalist!

As Carey stepped off his bike and into the arms of his friends, he quietly asked for some help in walking.

"I think I might have broken my foot," he said. But he never stopped smiling. On this night, for Carey, it was a small price to pay.

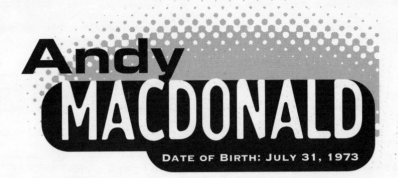

Andy MACDONALD

DATE OF BIRTH: JULY 31, 1973

If you think Andy Macdonald is nothing more than Tony Hawk's wing man, you're dead wrong. Oh, sure, Tony is unquestionably the most famous and successful skateboarder in history. And he has teamed up with Andy to win a record six consecutive X Games gold medals in the vert doubles competition. But "Andy Mac" is no slouch. In fact, he's one of the best skaters on the planet. He's the only man ranked in the top ten in both vert and street. He's also won six consecutive World Cup Skateboarding overall points championships.

To Andy, though, those are minor accomplishments. He has bigger goals in mind. Like securing health insurance and better earnings for his fellow skaters. And being a role model for kids. In 1999, for example, Andy became the first athlete invited to present a public service announcement at the White House on behalf of the Partnership for a Drug-Free America. In a sport that often seems to reward radical and even self-destructive behavior, Andy is as clean as they come. He doesn't smoke cigarettes, drink alcohol or coffee, or take drugs of any kind. He doesn't even eat red meat. All he does is skate…and win.

• •

"A lot of my time now goes into the business of skateboarding. But it all comes down to one thing: every day I'm going to be somewhere in the world riding my skateboard, which is all that I have ever wanted to do."

• •

"Some skaters raise their eyebrows at Andy or call him dorky," Steve Caballero, another professional skater, told *Sports Illustrated*. "But everyone respects the way he skates. No one is having a greater influence on skating."

A native of Boston, Andy started skating

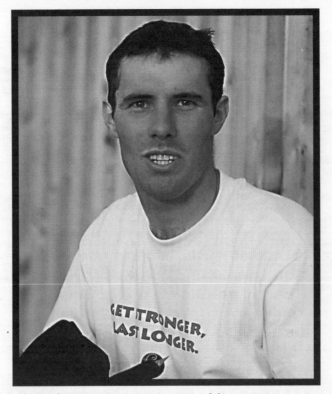

when he was seven years old, using a tiny banana board that was barely wide enough for his tiny feet. He didn't get a real board until he was 12, when his mother decided that skateboarding was probably safer than football.

"She probably thought it was just going to be a phase, you know?" Andy recalls.

Some phase. Nearly two decades later Andy is still skating with the energy and enthusiasm of a kid. He's one of the wealthiest men in skateboarding, with a long list of endorsements and private business interests. Not that it came easily, of course. Andy has worked as hard as anyone to build a career in extreme sports.

In his early teens he gave up his other athletic interests (swimming, basketball, gymnastics) so that he could devote more time to skating. Every day when he got home from school Andy would grab his board and head out to a local park or just skate in the street for hours on end. In time he developed into a pretty good skater. He won a few amateur contests in New England, and although the victories didn't exactly make Andy a household name, they did give him a dose of confidence.

But Andy knew he'd never reach his potential if he remained in the Northeast, where snow blanketed the ground and made skating virtually impossible six months of the year. There was, after all, a reason most of the best skaters chose to live in California and other warm-weather states. So, shortly after he graduated from high school, Andy packed up his stuff, threw it in the back of an old station wagon, and drove to San Diego.

"If you want to be an actor, you go to Hollywood, right?" Andy told the *Daily News Record*. "Well, if you want to be a skateboarder, you go to Southern California. That's where the whole industry is."

Andy arrived with 50 bucks in his pocket, no contacts, and no job prospects. The odds of him lasting more than a few weeks in California seemed long. But Andy was determined. He

A COUPLE THINGS YOU SHOULD KNOW

1. Andy almost never watches TV. In fact, until a couple years ago, when Tony Hawk bought him one so that he could watch videos of their performances, Andy didn't even own a television set.

2. Andy has a real fire pole in his house. It leads from his bedroom to his garage.

applied for jobs at convenience stores and restaurants, hoping to earn enough money to support his skating dream. But no one wanted to hire him. Eventually he did find work, although not exactly the type he had expected. Andy got a job at Sea World. He dressed up as Shamu the killer whale and walked around all day shaking hands (or fins!) with visitors.

Fortunately, Andy has always had a sense of humor, which helped him endure the hard times in those early years. By 1994 Andy had landed his first endorsement contract. It wasn't for much money, but it was enough to live on. From that moment on, Andy was a full-time professional skater.

"When I first started, I basically went to contests so that I could make enough money to go to the next contest," he says. "I was just trying to get by."

Andy's career took a dramatic turn for the better at the 1996 X Games in Newport, Rhode Island, where he upset Tony Hawk in the vert finals. Later that year he captured his first world championship. Since then Andy has accumulated a roomful of hardware, including an amazing

11 X Games medals, eight of them gold. In October of 1999 he also earned a spot in the *Guinness Book of World Records* by jumping 52 feet, 10.5 inches on his skateboard. The following spring he shattered his own record, clearing 56 feet, 10.75 inches.

Those exploits, many of which were televised nationally, brought Andy a flood of attention and dozens of sponsorship offers. Some he accepted, and they naturally made his life easier. But Andy rejected a lot of offers, too. To this day he refuses to endorse companies that produce tobacco or alcohol. And he won't work for any firm whose products do not meet his rigid standards.

"I make my choices based on moral principles," Andy says matter-of-factly. "I have to be able to use the products I endorse."

Andy is obviously a man of integrity. That's one of the reasons he is so respected by fans and skaters alike. Andy feels fortunate to have had so many opportunities in life, and now he wants to use his power and influence to make things better for others. Specifically, he wants to improve conditions for the skateboarders throughout the world.

A TRUE HERO

Andy's idol is not an athlete. The man he most admires is Mohandas Gandhi, the Indian political and spiritual leader whose devotion to peace and social justice inspired millions of followers. Andy says Gandhi's autobiography is his favorite book, and he tries to use Gandhi as a role model in his own life.

"That's who I look up to," Andy says. "He's a great inspiration to me. I wish I could be half the man he was."

"I want to make this a legitimate sport," Andy told the *Philadelphia Inquirer.* "I want people to know that there are skaters who are every bit as talented and gifted as the baseball players who are making millions of dollars."

Andy isn't just trying to recruit new fans for skateboarding. He's actively working on behalf of his fellow competitors. As a board member of the United Professional Skateboarders Association, Andy is devoted to such fundamental issues as increasing prize money at contests and providing health insurance to athletes.

Andy is old enough that he can envision a day when he won't be able to compete for gold medals at the X Games. But he can't imagine that skating won't forever be a part of his life. He considers himself a skating activist, and he won't rest until everyone understands what he already knows: that skateboarding is the coolest sport around.

"Skateboarding has limitless possibilities," Andy says. "It's bigger than ever now. Stereotypes are being broken. Kids can say, 'I want to be a pro skater,' and chances are their dad is a skater and he's cool with that. Fifteen years ago, many parents were against skate-boarding. It wasn't seen as a sport, and no one thought you could have a career as a skater. Now it's a massive industry."

Andy pauses and laughs. "I want to see more public skate parks, and I hope that one day there will be a skate park next to every empty tennis court that people don't use anymore because they're all out skating."

Ryan NYQUIST

DATE OF BIRTH: MARCH 6, 1979

While pioneers Mat Hoffman and Dave Mirra tend to get most of the headlines, another athlete has captured the attention of bicycle stunt fans. His name is Ryan Nyquist, and he is perhaps the most explosive rider in freestyle BMX. He's also one of the most versatile.

Short, but powerfully built (5-foot-6, 150 pounds), Ryan has a remarkable ability to control his bike on all types of surfaces and courses. Although dirt jumping is his specialty, he is gifted at park and vert riding, as well. At the 2000 X Games, for example, he was the only rider to qualify for the finals in all three freestyle events, and he's struck X Games gold in both dirt and park. In 2001 he won one of the most prized titles in BMX: the overall Bike

Stunt Series championship in park.

So, even though there's nothing Ryan enjoys more than a few hours of intense training in the dirt, he takes pride in the fact that he is one of the most complete athletes in the sport. As long as he gets to make a living as a professional rider, Ryan is happy. More than one observer has noted that Ryan always seems to have a smile on his face, even in the middle of a stressful competition.

"You shouldn't be out there if you're not having fun," he says. "It's miserable if you're out there thinking, 'I have to do this, but I really don't want to.' Sometimes the training gets hard at this level, but for the most part I just try to have a good time and be lighthearted and sing songs to myself and stuff."

That positive attitude has made Ryan one of the most popular extreme sports stars. Fans like to watch him compete and perform, especially when he's executing one of his trademark backflips. And other riders like to hang with him, not only because Ryan helps them improve, but also because he's fun to be around. Ryan grew up in Los Gatos, California, but now lives in Greenville, North Carolina. Greenville has become a popular gathering spot for BMX riders, including such outstanding pros as Dave Mirra and Allan Cooke. So Ryan always has an assortment of talented training partners.

"There's about a dozen pros in town, so it's

pretty cool," Ryan says. "There's a lot of people to ride with and we're all constantly pushing each other. It makes it fun, because you're always learning new things."

Unlike some of his extreme sports counterparts, Ryan was not a child prodigy. You know, the kind of kid who was leaping over cars in the backyard when he was in kindergarten. He

● ●

"Motivation is the key to getting better. It's not always the people you ride with. It's how badly you want to excel. Stick with it and make sure it's fun, because if it's fun, that's pretty much all you need."

● ●

was just a normal kid who liked to ride his bike all over town. There were no skate parks or vert ramps or any other places where kids were encouraged to practice alternative sports in Los Gatos. So Ryan settled for jumping curbs and bushes and generally just behaving like a little daredevil.

In middle school Ryan met some other kids

GOAL-ORIENTED

If you had asked Ryan when he was in middle school to name his favorite sport, he probably wouldn't have said BMX. In fact, Ryan was a soccer fanatic who played competitively for more than a decade. He still follows the sport and wishes he had time to join a league.

who liked to ride BMX bikes. They took Ryan to a dirt patch outside of town where they had built a series of hills and jumps, and together they rode for hours. At that point Ryan was hooked.

"I started hanging out with these other guys, just riding and having fun and trying to learn new tricks," Ryan recalls. "Sure, you take crashes once in a while, but you're young, man. It's like, you crash and you get this huge scab and you're like, 'Yeahhh!'"

By the time he was 15, Ryan had successfully executed his first big-time trick: turning

360 degrees in the air on his bike. A year later he started practicing backflips off a ramp set up at the edge of a lake. That didn't work too well, however, so Ryan built a pit and filled it with foam rubber and old mattresses to soften his fall. Before long he had mastered some of the most difficult tricks in BMX. So he decided to turn professional.

"Jumping was just a fun thing to do," Ryan says. "I enjoyed doing it in my spare time, and then it gradually escalated into competing and then doing it for a living. I never expected it to get this far."

Maybe not, but once he made a commitment to freestyle BMX, Ryan quickly became one of the best in the world. In 1998, when he was only 19 years old, he was the overall dirt circuit champion. And he defended that title in 1999. In 2000 Ryan won his first X Games bicycle stunt gold medal, taking first place in the dirt competition. With his backflip barspins and a full 720 (two consecutive 360-degree turns on a single jump), Ryan set a new standard for dirt jumping. It's hard enough to complete tricks like that on a vert ramp, where

COPING WITH FEAR

Ryan is an honest guy. Although he's able to conquer the fear that confronts most freestyle BMX riders, he admits that there are some things that make his knees weak. Like heights. That's right—a man who earns his living by doing flips on his bike has a fear of heights.

"On the bike I'm all right," Ryan explains with a laugh. "But when it comes to standing on the edge of a building or anything high, I can't handle it."

the surface is smooth and hard and consistent. On dirt, it's almost impossible. But Ryan made it look almost easy.

Ryan added a silver medal in dirt at the 2001 X Games. But if anyone thought he was strictly a one-dimensional rider, they were sadly mistaken. Before the year was out, Ryan won the Bike Stunt Series title in park. And at the 2002 X Games in Philadelphia, he was easily the most impressive freestyle rider in town.

Sure, Dave Mirra was his usual awesome self in the vert competition. And, yes, Mat "The Condor" Hoffman did land a 900. But nobody demonstrated greater versatility than Ryan Nyquist.

In addition to taking another silver medal in the dirt jumping competition, Ryan won the gold medal in park. And he accomplished this feat while using a bike borrowed from another rider. Seriously! After Ryan busted his bike in the middle of his first run, he was forced to turn to his friend and Greenville neighbor, Allan Cooke, for help. Cooke didn't mind and happily offered Ryan a ride. Amazingly enough, Ryan then turned in one of the best performances of his life. He nailed every trick on his second run, including a perfect 720.

"I found some good lines on the course and I landed everything that I wanted to," Ryan said afterward. "Allan's bike felt pretty good. I should have tried it during dirt jumping. Then maybe I would have gotten the gold there, too."

He was just kidding, of course. Ryan was happy with his effort and the results it produced. After all, freestyle BMX has already given him more than he ever imagined it would. He gets to ride a bike for a living. And it is, for Ryan at least, a pretty good living. In addition to the prize money he earns, Ryan has several lucrative sponsorship deals with such companies as Haro Bikes and Adidas. And his talent and personality have helped him earn prominent roles in a pair of extreme sports documentaries: *Miracle Boy and Nyquist* (about Ryan's friendship with Dave Mirra) and *Ultimate X* (an eye-popping IMAX film about the X Games).

But Ryan takes it all in stride. It isn't much of a stretch to say that even if there were no cameras, no crowds and no prize money, Ryan would still be out there somewhere on his bike.

Riding and smiling.

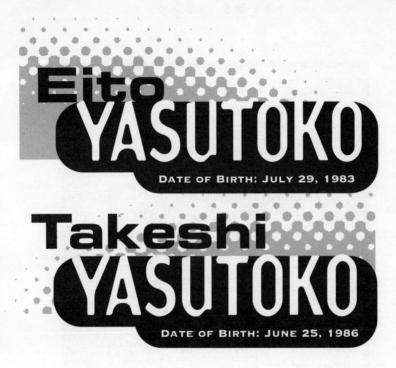

Eito YASUTOKO

DATE OF BIRTH: JULY 29, 1983

Takeshi YASUTOKO

DATE OF BIRTH: JUNE 25, 1986

Tennis has the Williams sisters. In-line skating has the Yasutoko brothers.

Venus and Serena are two dazzling young athletes who seem to have reinvented the sport of tennis. They are fierce rivals on the court, and best friends off it, despite the fact that they have very different personalities (Venus is quiet, serious. Serena is playful and outgoing).

Takeshi Yasutoko

They were introduced to the game at an early age by their father. And now it seems the only time either one loses is when she faces her sibling.

● ●

"If Eito does a big trick, I won't do the same trick. I will compete against him with a different trick. Some tricks I can do and he can't. And some he can do that I can't."
–Takeshi

● ●

Sounds a lot like the story of Eito and Takeshi Yasutoko, young pioneers of the vert ramp and the most dominant performers in the sport of aggressive in-line skating. Together they have amassed seven X Games medals, including three gold. Older brother Eito's athleticism and technical skill, combined with Takeshi's artistry, has made the duo nearly unbeatable in competitive events and enormously popular in demonstrations. Despite the fact that in-line skating is not very big in their native land (they were born and raised in Osaka, Japan), the Yasutoko brothers have become worldwide celebrities among followers of alternative sports.

"We always aim for the top position," explains Eito. "It's not just a matter of self-satisfaction. We also want to please the fans."

There is one very significant way in which the Yasutoko brothers differ from the Williams sisters: they were born into their sport. Richard Williams was just a father who liked tennis and taught his daughters how to play. Yuki Yasutoko and his wife, Tomoko, have been

Safety First

The Yasutoko brothers do some wild things on the vert ramp, but they always try to protect themselves as much as possible. Eito's advice to young skaters? "Those who want to get involved in this sport should always take precautions. Wear the safety gear, because accidents can happen at any time."

skating most of their lives. In fact, they are former roller disco dancers who often competed in contests! The Yasutoko family business is a skate park, so Eito and Takeshi naturally spent a lot of time there when they were growing up. Each laced up his first pair of traditional roller skates when he was barely old enough to walk. And each soon graduated to in-line skating, which offered the potential for greater control, speed and creativity.

Soon the brothers were competing in contests and doing their best to live up to the Yasutoko name. That's no small task. After all, the Yasutokos are known as the "first skate family of Japan." And, to be honest, the boys at first weren't even sure they wanted to carry that burden. But when they left Japan and witnessed the popularity of in-line skating around the globe, they quickly changed their minds.

"We didn't really want to skate at first," Eito told *Sports Illustrated for Kids*. "But we had to because our parents were skaters. Then, around 1995, we went to our first competition in the United States. I saw many good skaters, and I really got hooked."

Eito, who is three years older than Takeshi, was naturally the first of the Yasutoko brothers to make a name for himself on the international scene. In 1998 he finished fourth in vert at the X Games, and in 1999 he not only won the gold medal in vert, but also teamed up with Takeshi and another skater to take third in the vert triples competition. Eito was only 16 and one of the youngest athletes to win an X Games medal that summer. Of course, Takeshi was only 13. He was the youngest medalist in the

• •

"Feeling scared is no excuse for not trying new tricks. I have a sense of responsibility because I am influencing the world of skating."
–Eito

• •

entire history of the X Games!

Ever since that day, Eito hasn't had to look far to find his main competition. All he has to do is look right over his shoulder.

"I'm the big brother, so I'm supposed to beat him," Eito told the *Cincinnati Enquirer*. "But the truth is, I think Takeshi is better than me, because he has so much natural talent. I always have to practice a lot. He doesn't."

To which Takeshi responds: "I do practice. But Eito does more research, both in skating

Eito Yasutoko

UNIVERSAL LANGUAGE

Neither Eito nor Takeshi speaks English (their interviews are conducted with the help of a translator). But that hasn't prevented them from becoming enormously popular in the United States and Europe. In fact, both brothers say they're much more famous in America than they are at home in Japan.

and in everyday life. Sometimes I wonder if that's necessary."

Despite their common passion for in-line skating, the Yasutoko brothers are actually different in many ways. Eito is taller and more muscular. His moves on the vert ramp reflect his strength and power. He approaches the sport with seriousness and determination. In fact, there is no aggressive in-line skater who is more aggressive than Eito. That may explain why he's had so many injuries, including numerous sprains and broken bones.

Takeshi, on the other hand, seems to glide

up and down the vert ramp. Smaller and lighter, he is almost birdlike in appearance. Instead of attacking the ramp, Takeshi plays it like a musical instrument. And the results can be breathtaking. No other skater soars as high as Takeshi, and no one else makes it all seem quite so effortless.

There are other differences. Eito is fanatical about skating. He has almost no interest in any other sports. Takeshi, meanwhile, is a big sports fan who closely follows baseball. Their taste in music differs sharply, too. Eito listens to hard rock while practicing and competing, and then mellows out to such new-age performers as Enya when he's hanging out at home. Takeshi? He prefers Japanese hip-hop.

Individual preferences aside, the Yasutoko brothers share a common goal. They want to be the best in the world, and to elevate the sport of in-line skating. So they work together in practice every day, sometimes for as long as eight hours. With their father standing nearby, they coax each other to new heights. And, believe it or not, they almost never bicker or fight.

"Takeshi is a very good skater because of his brother," notes Yuki Yasutoko. "They are healthy rivals, pushing each other to be better skaters and to be number one."

So do the boys *ever* fight? You know, the way most brothers do?

"Sure," Eito says with a smile. "We fight every day on the vert ramp. Sometimes I teach him, and sometimes he teaches me."

"We have our troubles," Takeshi admits. "But we try to have fun skating."

If fun can be measured in trophies, then the Yasutoko brothers are having a blast. Eito repeated as vert champion in 2000, narrowly beating out Takeshi for the gold medal. In 2002 they switched places, with Takeshi winning the gold and Eito settling for silver. They stood head and shoulders above their rivals on the awards platform, just as they stand head and shoulders above the rest of the skating world.

They're not giving up that position anytime soon. Eito says he wants to become a "legendary" skater. And both brothers say they plan to compete until they're at least 30 years old. After that, they'd like to build skate parks and promote the sport in Japan.

"We want to train young skaters and groom world champions," Eito says.

Who knows? By that time there may even be another champion in the Yasutoko household. You see, Eito and Takeshi have a little sister named Anna. She's five years old, and she already knows her way around a halfpipe.